Night's Glass Table

Karen Zelas

Interactive Press
Brisbane

Interactive Press
an imprint of IP (Interactive Publications Pty Ltd)
Treetop Studio • 9 Kuhler Court
Carindale, Queensland, Australia 4152
sales@ipoz.biz
ipoz.biz/IP/IP.htm

First published by IP in 2012
© Karen Zelas, 2012

Printed in 12 pt Cochin on 16 pt Helvetica Neue.

National Library of Australia
Cataloguing-in-Publication entry:

Author: Zelas, Karen

Title: Night's glass table / Karen Zelas.

ISBN: 9781921869914 (pbk.)

Subjects: Love poetry.
           Grief--Poetry.
           Death--Poetry.
           New Zealand poetry.

Dewey Number: NZ821.3

Interactive Press

Night's Glass Table

Karen Zelas lives in quake-struck Christchurch. A former psychiatrist and psychotherapist, she returned to university, taking creative writing papers at Canterbury University in preparation for giving up her day job. Since 2004, her poetry has been increasingly widely published within New Zealand, including in **Landfall**, **Poetry New Zealand** *and* **Takahē**, *and broadcast on radio. It has also appeared in Australian ezines* **Snorkel** *and* **Eclecticism** *and recently been blogged by* **Interlitq** *(UK). Several anthologies contain her work.*

Having an interest in the visual presentation of poetry, Karen participated, in April 2007, in an exhibition entitled **feathers unfettered**, *featuring her series of poems about native birds of New Zealand. The exhibition was mounted with artist Galina Kim and quilter Sue Spigel, in Christchurch. In 2009, she was the recipient of a Creative Communities grant.*

Karen is editor of the anthology **Crest to Crest: Impressions of Canterbury, prose and poetry** *(Wily Publications, 2009).*

Her first novel **Past Perfect** *[view at www.KarenZelas.com] was published by Wily Publications in 2010, and is to be released in ebook editions by Interactive Publications this year.*

For the last five years, Karen has been Fiction Editor of **Takahē** *literary magazine [view at www.takahe.org.nz] and chairs the Takahē Collective Board. She is married with children, grandchildren and child-substitute: a miniature poodle.*

Interactive Press
The Literature Series

for Henry, Damian and Martin

Acknowledgements

Front Cover Image: Henry Zelas

Jacket Design: David Reiter

Author Photo (frontispiece): Frances Zelas

Author Photo (back cover): Henry Zelas

Some of the following poems (or earlier versions) have been published in *a fine line, Blackmail Press, bravado, Eclecticism, Landfall, Pasture, Poetry NZ, Snorkel, Takahē, The Press,* the New Zealand Poetry Society anthology, *Before the Sirocco* (2008) and blogged by *Interlitq.* My sincere thanks to the editors of these publications.

I am indebted to the many poets whose works set my imagination racing, inspiring some of my own poems. Specific acknowledgements are made in the Notes section.

To the poets and other writers with whom I have shared searching and inspiring discussion in critique groups and workshops over the last few years, I say thank you. Their criticism, support and friendship have extended and sustained me in my writing. I am particularly grateful to Joanna Preston and, in the recent past, to Siobhan Harvey and Claire Hero for sharing their wisdom. Also to Joanna for reading and commenting upon this manuscript.

As always, my love and thanks to my husband Henry for his tolerance, and, well, for everything.

Contents

My House Has Many Rooms   3

... through tinted glass or eye
Lemon Tree   7
Awakening   8
Summer in Ossetia   9
Aftermath   11
Expiration   12
Foundations   13
Mother's Jacket   14

Deep in the womb there is a room for you ...
Azimuth   17
Out of Shadow   18
Re-vision   19
Vin de Villanelle   20
Leavening   21
Giacometti's Fancy   22
Shortcut   23
Windfalls   24
On Losing Her Way   25

The study's full of fertile loam ...
Digging Deep   29
Deafness in the Garden of the Blind   30
Migration   31
Air Born   33
Behind the Bus   34
Mrs Popper's Sunhat   35
After Shock   37
Moscow Underground   38
Upheaval   39
Wings   40

The gallery's as long as many lives …
From the Dead 43
Dealing with It 44
Grandmother's Grave 45
Odyssey 46
A Long Time Coming 47
Eclipsed 48
She-wolf 49
The Best Money Could Buy 50
Chekhov's Birthday 51

For reflection, enter bathroom calm …
Out of the Whiteness 55
What Is Yet To Come 56
The Weight of Calves 59
Dawn Parade 61
Approach 62
Unsaid 63
Small Islands of Difference 64
This Is How It Feels … 66
In July I Think of Him 67

In the bedroom, shadows scud …
Congress 71
Convergence 72
Loving You 73
A Song Sung 74
Extraordinary Lightness 75
On Your Toes 76
Breakfast in Berlin 77
Love 78
I Too Have Loved 79

Notes 82

Night's Glass Table

My House Has Many Rooms

in which I wander. It will take a life
to complete the circuit. Refuge
where least expected, inspiration in a hook,
a nook, a look through tinted glass or eye.

Deep in the womb there is a room for you
and you and whomsoever I choose
to shelter. Sink into downy clouds.
Sip on evening's fruity brew.
Admire the view.

The study's full of fertile loam I tend.
Words come to feed, flit and hover,
beat wings on one another, poise sometimes
upon the page, dusting colour; filamentous
legs and pulsing thorax.

The gallery's as long as many lives.
We glide through time, examine sepia faces,
sounds trapped in vinyl, pink leather
baby shoes, grandpa's opera hat and glasses, all
dimly lit, yet vibrant.

For reflection, enter bathroom calm.
Still pool or steaming fall. The colour sky
in all my moods; mountains
I must climb, chasms that yawn,
by which to mark my stride.

In the bedroom, shadows scud
across a counterpane of tussock;
silhouette of hip and rib and thigh.
I lie alone where the hawk ascends. Below
the valley's dam is full, begins to overflow.

… through tinted glass or eye

Lemon Tree

It thrived in the Garden of Eden.
Fig and date and pomegranate, sweetmeats
in the cradle of man. Succulent flesh
to suck from teeth, between
boredom and self-stimulation.

A spare rib changed all that.

By the time Lucifer kicked down the wall
so all might enter, innocence had flown,
a white, scented petal on the *hamsin*.
He tainted the flesh to celebrate
so none who tasted could smile.

Come with me, whore. See
how the lemon tree lifts its head,
yes, here. With camel gaze, dares
fingers to pluck its fruit. Even the oil cuts.
Don't temper the juice with honey.

Awakening

He sat high on a branch, bare
legs dangling above her head
so she couldn't look up
in case she saw what she was not
supposed to. She was in the dark
and he those few years older.

Bet you don't know what 'fuck' means
he laughed a laugh that conjured up
all those scary stories
those cautionary tales
grownups read to children.

She dipped the comb into the rusty can
of water, ran it through the forelock
of her russet calf, curled a cowlick,
stared into its liquid eyes wishing
it could always stay this way.

Do too she said

although she didn't
know the meaning of the word
she realised things

could never be the same again.
Even calves were made somehow.

Summer in Ossetia

bewildered

you raise a bare arm
in farewell perhaps

or a summons to set in reverse
the process of destruction
make the egg-shell pieces
of rubble leap together

reconstitute your home
the familiar street
the corner store
the walls
where women leaned
on one another

a stubborn vine
holds fast
to a façade at the end
of the lane   three
empty window frames

this dust bowl holds
the sounds of your children
in the shadows
memories pinioned

your father's last breath
your daughter's first cry
trapped beneath that pile
of tortured wood

the bed where you lay with your husband
(gone to another woman)
collapsed with the top floor (and your heart)
into the basement

your sons gone too now
to thwart
the bear's wanderlust …

the dust clings
grits the teeth
occludes the sun

it is a summer too dry for tears

Aftermath

it was not we but a raptor
dropped that bomb

knocked into submission
the yellow peril
a bald statement

hatred knew no bounds
nor fear

stories whispered (or not)
of men bent like bamboo canes
hollow   crippled

captor and captured
never again to sleep

the sleep of childhood

Expiration

She raises her eyes.
A breath in the night. A sigh.
Leaves her sewing
in favour of the window, the frame
illuminated, the glass reflecting her fear,
a woman in black against black
already in mourning. She knows
there are hills out there, bound
with a shingle road, wound tightly, comfort
in invisible form, smooth curves.
She knows, too, that a man is unlikely
to survive an explosion inside a steel
shell beneath the sea's surface.
That pressure bursts cells; that water
will breach. Worse still, she sees fire.
She hopes it was quick. But this
does not preclude his loitering in the corner
of the room, in the corner of her eye,
humming their tune and winking at her, that lopsided grin.
Nor smother the firefly of light wavering in darkness
winding towards her, nor the certainty

Foundations

They came with trucks and concrete-pump and
traced the plan on tamped base-course.
Each room defined in relief –
like the outline of the Roman camp
below Masada, the desert mountain
on which I sweated, gazing down
as no doubt the besieged
sweated and gazed down
before taking the only path out …

I step inside the border, pause
in space, as if again exploring
that ancient site. Levitate
into crisp blue air and float in mind
through hallway, bedrooms, stair

They will add block layers bound
with steel, then membrane, foam,
a strengthened concrete pad to form
a firm foundation – like the Romans
– on this restless land

Minor shakes cause no concern
but when *the big one* comes
we plan
          to ride the wave

Mother's Jacket

I touch the nap where her fingers
lingered, the jacket snuggled to my ears
strange
it should fit us both
when she was so much
smaller

strange so small a garment
should transmit such warmth
protect so well
from buffeting winds
and the snags and stabs
of unexpected thorns

Deep in the womb there is a room for you ...

Azimuth

I came upon her one summer night,
the rustle of heat trapped in dry grass, trees
heavy with sibilance. She floated
above the end paddock, full and huge
in a notch of black hills.
No visible tether; round
as a party balloon, but not of this world.
A widow's veil muted her flushed complexion,
thin luminous smile growing as if a flame
were held beneath her chin. Sinister.

The earth and I, backs to the sun. An eerie glow.
I faltered, out of alignment. Small wonder
I didn't know her – celestial canons show her
last widowed at summer solstice
near 400 years ago.

Out of Shadow

Bush-dark night, the morepork's
plaintive call

more-pork   more-pork

a sob that carries in empty air.
He begs and begs

– for food, for love? Unlike you,
he knows to ask

more-pork   more-pork

Hearing, your wound
splits wide, reveals

the hollow she has left,
and I say there's

always one more place
at night's glass table

and we watch the glow of dawn
reflecting

Re-vision

There is a moment, somewhere, when I
see you. Truly see you. A gift.
Before a glass,

           a Renaissance self-
portrait.
Maybe in a courtyard, a Gothic arch

or by a Roman column – the old so new –
unruly curls snaking, your father's smile,
Sicilian sun.   A fishing harbour, gulls
rising through blue, many steps, and you
carry my burden. Ionian light
and Jason searching

             for himself.

Or perhaps, in relief
against a white wall; always white walls.
Blue-and-white tiles and men mending nets.
The voice of the market. Bull-fight roar
in the wind.

Twin iron beds in a whitewashed room. A fan
to cut hot heavy air. A small table:
bread on white paper, a knife
beside cheese, sharing stories
and red wine, thicker than water.

Vin de Villanelle

Wine bottles empty by the door
remains of repast on the table.
In this life, who could ask for more?

You arrived unbid and with you bore
olives, cheese, all you were able,
a wine bottle, beside the door.

Another from the fridge I draw.
You take a chair, slip off your sable –
in this life, who could ask for more?

We share our loves – you start to bore –
it's hard to tease out fact from fable.
Another bottle by the door.

Your shadow stretches across the floor,
one more drink and you slip your cable.
In this life who could ask for more?

Old friends' debris – not a chore.
I await the next time, truly, Mabel.
Wine bottles empty by the door.
In this life, who could ask for more?

Leavening

When all this is over, said the soldier,
I mean to retreat, where nobody
will have an inkling about my special
pursuits, and life is mainly about living.

I intend to bake bread, at least as yeasty
as the sun bursting above the horizon,
leavening the new everyday. I want to sing
at dawn, kneading the dough, listening
to the waking notes of a thrush
and the throaty burble of the predator
crouched low near the bake-house door.

I want to meet my love
where the river in spring breaches
its banks, and the yellowhammer
finds dry wisps woven through fallen
trees, where darkness makes me tremble
only with anticipation
and the past
is allowed to decay on the far shore.

Giacometti's Fancy

a roomful of women
ranked
arms pinned to skinny hips
chins tilted
in submission
made

not in man's image
but his fancy

*

submission

or silent defiance
in a world of men
where thinness
is a pearl
to be cultivated

at a price

*

is it hindsight
that sees
in the tilt
of chin a spark
that ignites
lights
their daughters
onwards?

Shortcut

taking a shortcut through the park
I see a woman
in a combat suit and bicycle helmet
on a swing:

      up   *down*
      legs out   *legs in*

her bicycle rests against the slide
our breath
mists the grey air
and I muse
on what drives adults to play
children's games

I envision small sandaled feet
high in the sky
breeze fluttering her skirt
like a prayer flag, and wonder

what has happened between then and now

Windfalls

I scoop them from the ground, soft carpet
of detritus, searching for the firm
and yellowing green.
Each sits in my palm. Fulsome. I cup
cold fingers around another, half buried, find
the underside a squish of brown
and let it lie.
        The last of the summer crop hangs
tempting from above, but I've been sent
to gather windfalls and make the best of them.
I shall excise all wounded flesh, make
pear and walnut chutney in my mother's pan.
Wait six weeks to know

whether
        bruised fruit can be rescued.

On Losing Her Way

No fanfare, no gods, a bloody afterglow.

In real time, in the winter of her life,
haze drifts in, wraps a comfortless cloak;
a damp sea mist, pierced by the occasional
glimmer of an anchor-light, briefly orienting.

It's easy to mourn in winter, hearing her
groan under the weight of the past –
all the cares of the world bending,
and knowing there will be no respite,

no going back to summer lightness
with the future a fiery radiance at the end
of a long, long day.

Not remembering
                    the happiness.

The study's full of fertile loam …

Digging Deep

I'd like
to pen a poem about my grandfather, about
how I toiled beside him as a child
our breaths misting grey autumn air,
the blade of his large spade slicing
the veggie patch under the punch
of my gumbooted heel; how we
dug-in last year's compost
from behind the shed; how he taught
me to dig a neat furrow, bury
seed potatoes deep, bedding them in;
how together we mounded them. Bent
a shoulder to fork the first
for the Christmas roast. About his
green thumb, how he taught me
all I know. But
to be truthful, I never knew
my grandfather.

Deafness in the Garden of the Blind

you are sighted yet do not see
not deaf, though you seem

unmoved by vibration
of butterfly wings

through herbaceous borders
a flit of gossamer orange

fragile
I rub rosemary between my fingers

sage
you do not notice

in another land
conflict erupts

a plane roars overhead

you're unperturbed

Migration

we missed you this year godwits
massed across the sands
in rows, faces into the wind waiting
for the right moment for take-off

your long fine beaks had sliced
the summer shallows fuelling
for the long flight, your own
pilots navigators and engine power

*

so many came steerage
to these shores knowing they
would not see kith nor kin
nor Home again

but you slender wanderer
migrate in the certainty
next season will see you
return to an Alaskan summer
sunlight and sex

*

we found a few stragglers
in the estuary, reluctant perhaps
while late summer sun stings
anticipating the long haul
China en route

maybe next year
we'll time it right
see your sleek bodies
lift, wings darkening the sky
heading north west

light-seeking

Air Born

Going tandem makes it possible; I want to
fly, a feather, a bird's eye, but could never
step alone into this emptiness. His
confidence is contagious. I pay the fee
to be reborn. Cool air slipstreams.
We swoop. We soar. I fight to keep my
heart within my chest. The mountain falls
away. 'Slipping,' I yell. 'Hold on,'
he shouts, then soft, 'Forgive me' –
words on the wind, as Daedalus
drifts from reach and I plunge
wings folded like a gannet
                              down
                                    down
till the ripcord in my brain yanks
and the land spreads like melted wax

Behind the Bus

swerve left, or not?
patience, or push ahead?

your *split-second decision*

defines the moment
and the next, the next
the difference
between a future and

your *recurring image*:

the earth heaves
the bus is crushed in

your ivory face, a façade
falling
a veil of dust, a limb

rim of cycle wheel; red
hair spilling
the last crush of breath

the pain
        of living

Mrs Popper's Sunhat

It was the rays that drove her
across the world to a land she believed
unplagued by electrons, by air
thick with ionic detritus that charges
rogue cells to spawn their malign likeness,
addles heart, brain, liver, spleen, crushing
the meek and healthy.

It had been the dishes on the roof –
their electron-swords piercing the ceiling.
The kitchen, the bedroom, the duvet pulled over
her head. They found her. She saw their invisible
shimmer through industrial fog. She trembled
in her lounge, waiting

to ring her daughters – again – to
explain – again – her need
to escape. No one listened. She pulled her soft sunhat
over her ears for protection and studied
the world on tremulous pages ...

She explained all this in the far-off green land,
a place free to wander in silk and in lace, like a bride
stepping out, a new life beginning. She slept
with no fear. This she told the officials
and asked for asylum.

They came, in the end, not the rays
but the men, and sent her away, seeking safety
again. Her sunhat *regretfully*
lost in transition. There

lay the tragedy.

After Shock

Kinaesthesia: the sense of movement

An imprint shocked into your body. Still
it plucks dendrites, awakens a memory:
the anchored chair trembles; the firm floor
shifts. Disequilibrated equilibrist,

heel to toe, you step the lines of street,
searching for real: flesh and blood. Dust-
laden air drums an echo, the body an album.

Mannequins lean, odd angles, exposed
to the elements. Eyes fixed. Heaped glass and bricks.
A neon tube glimmers in Quinn's upper storey.
You walked out alive – you are still in your body.
Pinned in the rubble, a scrap of silk flutters;
a cat slinks low, seeks the way home.

Moscow Underground

She could have been painted by Boticelli.
I am wilting, exhausted from finding my way.
You await my return.

She stands apart from others, descending,
I, ride the escalator towards a strange street.
You, imagine me, lost in a foreign city?

Long twists of hair frame her face, chin
lifted in private rapture. I am anxious
about making you anxious.

One hand holds her dress under a swelling belly
while I transliterate Cyrillic script:
         КРАСНОПРЕСНСКАЯ
not wanting to lose myself, or you.

She rides the steel stairs like a partisan, the future
                    her promise and legacy.
I emerge from the underworld into the right street.
                         I will return,
soothe your brow, and tell you of Chekhov's
                      'tallboy' house.

Upheaval

He felt the thrust beneath his feet
      the roil, the boil of floorboards
heard the roar, a freight train
         hurtling out of control, the tilt
of his world, all his memories
               tumbling
                 from
                   high
                 places

And when the tremors stopped,
he picked a path through
the sharp fragments of his life,
paused in the door, anticipating
an aftershock. But there was only
silence, stillness,
as if none but he existed.

Emptiness. He was unprepared, dared not stir.
Dared not step into the void created in her wake.

All she'd said was, 'I'm leaving.'

Wings

Death comes fleet as a swallow,
soft wings folding about your shoulders,
quick beak combing the scrub of your moustache
as if the last breath may disturb a cloud of insects.

Grey your pallor, eyes as large as pinheads
in which I see myself walking away without you.

A magpie-swoop of hard black wings, the whirr,
pecking at my flesh for some small glittering token
– a pearl worried from a grain of sand;

gargled cries rattle along the empty road, straight
and rising, metal
reflecting heat and light, like a scimitar letting blood,
and all behind me
red.

The gallery's as long as many lives …

From the Dead

it feels wrong at first to tread on your faces
many-deep, thousands of faces

on approach, a sound like cattle-trucks
shunting, the point of departure

open-mouthed, rude-cut and rusted
faces tilt and shriek, metal on metal

our tread gives you voice, your screams
aired once more, thousands of, millions of

ssscccrrreeeaaammmsss
in the void

I tramp   I stamp   I weep –

a towering chimney of screams
and I hear
            each   voice

Dealing with It

We cleaned out Dad's garage
the day of his funeral

Mum, Jack and me

filled the boot of his baby-
blue Hillman Imp

went to the tip
as clouds gathered

That was the mourning
The afternoon

we committed him
to flames

and it poured

Grandmother's Grave

The washing hangs on the line, rigid
heartless. Granite-cold *in memoriam*,
slump of shoulders no longer there.

Your gravestone, when I found it that slow
spring morning in a foreign land,
stood erect, shoulders back, vigorous
as if there were life in you yet. As if

the polished slab had been set in error.
As if the grief in your wake
that charted the course for your young
daughter need never have been. Suddenly I
could feel your presence, see your husband
low at your feet, kissing
the flounced hem of your authority.

All my life you were known by your absence,
weight of sadness. But I found you, walled in
by brick and barbed wire coils. Shoulder
to shoulder; I released you,
free to wander in my mind, free
to live out the stolen years.

Odyssey

There are no maps
to ease the passage of the godless.

Already he is where none can follow. He
has climbed into this space, this cavern
in near-night, in the far-distance, driven. Cries
that crash in forests of memory. Hunter
and hunted,

and which is he? Obscured
in semi-darkness, crouched
head bent to bony knees,
eyes of landed fish. Nothing
can surprise him now. He is halfway
to star. Rasping breath. Rattle
of chest and chains. I would curl
beside him, head in the lap
that held me. Still
he cannot rest. One uncommitted soul.

I would call off the hunter and the hounds.
Silent, I plead his cause. We are connected
one last time.

Go easy, my father.

A Long Time Coming

I watch you slide
through golden links hung
like a fly-curtain across the maw;
even the metal's brilliance
can't disguise the reality
of your journey

perhaps he waits for you –
you've been a long time coming,
but then, he left too soon

and you like that devoted
duck, on and off the curb
exhorting her dead drake to rise
from the gutter …

the lengthened shadow
of a cross
        falling
          falling

never to touch
your flowerless box, no
six-pointed star to lead the way
the lick of flame
his gold ring
on your fourth finger still

Eclipsed

Thethrongthemusicthe anticipation
             She would have loved it:
stars piercing the black haze
Whoosh! a fiery trail skywards
bursts – stars eclipsed – and falls – Aaah!
Needles of light rain
on the sun-dry *marais*
             She would have loved it:
daughters side by side
heads tipped back, necks strained
Should they be holding hands
as they did then? – the sparklers
the Catherine wheels, Jumping Jacks and
Billy Thwaites throwing Tom Thumbs
under their skirts, leaping figures
against the bonfire
             She would have loved it:
the sky alive, a kaleidoscope of colour
at our feet its doppelganger
inverted in black water

And then it's done
             the last spark is out

She would have, she really would
have loved it

She-wolf

She prized a son, although she knew
sons are born to trouble. Understood self-
fulfilling prophesy, dared to challenge Fate –
even his name was gentle; she saw to that. Fostered
a creative germ that coiled and grew. Provided dolls
to help him find his yin. But,
What the – he preferred a truck; nailed sticks
to make a gun
and shoot her. Though he was a good boy
then; she'd hear no word against him.
Now
he's grown and doesn't mind,
yet still she knows her task: to lend him heart
to face his enemies
– and his friends –
stand tall, or if not, ignore
the beat against her ribs and with her
sharp mother-tongue slice
their misdirected youth;
but if she finds they've
slunk away, they've had their
fun at his expense,
she'll seek him out
wherever and however
beaten, say, *Give me that rope!*
Or if Hope has spread its wings, she'll
take a knife
and cut him down and hold him to her,
breathing life.

The Best Money Could Buy

Full-sized it was, and round,
tight as a belly, the bladder neck
tucked inside stiff leather lacing.

Tan and tanned, a sphere stitched
from bits of cowhide. Smeared with
dubbin, grit stuck like hope,

as if a basketball could buy their daughter
friendship. She was too young to see
disappointment knot their stomachs

when the ball dribbled into a corner
defeated
by her two left hands.

Chekhov's Birthday

My father was born on Chekhov's birthday. *I'd be
fifty today*, Chekhov said from the grave, and,
quite unrelated, my father popped out
in the antipodes. Spurious, you might think, to link
the two events; retrospectively difficult to avoid.
Both were observers of men – and women. A pithy
turn of phrase. Wry humour. My father, too,
might've been a famous writer, a famous
something … a famous anything … if he'd not had to
feed his family. Instead, he sold books, memorised
the telephone index. Today is their birthday; Father
would be one hundred-and-one. What might he
(and Chekhov) have done
with another forty-two years?

For reflection, enter bathroom calm …

Out of the Whiteness

a thing of great disorder
It would be easy to turn my back,
easier, in the moment, not
to see. To pretend reality is
of no account, shapeless,
a theatre of passing cloud;
some thing
to be dispersed
as the sun struggles
to pierce this heavy atmosphere,
not if, but when.

God knows I tried in my own way
in younger days, when, foolish, I believed
in myself – and in others. Expected
mankind would bow to reason.

But, again and again again
I flinch before repetitions,
though it is known
what can make a difference.

Now my hand cups a white bud
against the southerly. This is
all I can do.

What Is Yet To Come

i

blue night, the white coin of moon
anneals a path on thickening swirls
a slurry of frosted glass
the exact moment: fusion
of land and sea and icing up
of heart still the quickening beat
eyes pricked with crystals
the knowing what is yet to come

oh, my dear, I dare not conjure
your widowed countenance

there is no leaving now, the long night young
the howl of dogs, anticipation
tempered, the frozen moment exposed
plated; so little light

ii

the ponies stumble, snorts of steam
ice-up their balaclavas; spindle legs
in clefts, sleds overturned, wild eyes
man-haul, four to a sled; whiteout
feet placed blindly, the going
stronger than the return
cold stiffens the jaw, hunger weakens
not the spirit

... I may be some time

you feel my tread as you lie
where frost never thaws
ice splinters in your eyes
and in your ears
the distant groaning of the sea

iii

waves snap-frozen, crests
like frosting on his wedding cake
trapped in pack ice they hunker down
create a show of order and routine
remove the vital organs from their ship
its rimy carcass snares the fading light

he wedges wooden legs nearby, the lens
a frosted eye, the slow grind and thrust
against the hull, agony of wood and iron
the sickening shriek of splintering skin
mast, spars, like kindling, rise
and scatter; death-throes emplated

beyond endurance, the hardest thing:
to choose which images to break, which to save

iv

voices in permafrost   scream
of steel in ice-blue air
strewn fragments of body and wing
cut a tomb; the seared slope
of maunga in ghost-light rising
ice-cliffs a cathedral, translucent
flutes of organ

hushed whispers:

closure

water from Aoraki
the orchestrated litany
lies in crisp air, perpetual light, a koru
in memoriam

The Weight of Calves

A calf estimated to weigh
thirty million tonnes
split from the Tasman Glacier.
If this was its weight,
imagine if you can, its size, ice
more voluminous than water.

And imagine its age:
I'm told the residence time
of glacier water may tip
one million years. All
those old molecules, trapped
for aeons, waiting release
into Brownian motion.
The world's reservoirs
leaking. Greened plains lapped
by cattle. The weight.

The birth of a calf is assisted
by gravity. Maternal groans
as the glacier labours through rock
and the calf   drops,
torn from terminal ice. An echoing crash.
A wave. Turquoise light. Hard
shards slice water. The calf
part-submerged, melting. Freshwater
mingles with saline.

Calving into water causes a splash;
into oceans, raises the level. Collapse
the ice sheets and tides will lift
six metres perhaps. Think of that.

                    Cows and calves
where they never should be.
Weighing heavy.

Dawn Parade

the rains are over
                    mud reminds
the air heavy with song
and moisture misting

the billabong still
water tannin-black
                    a mirror
water lilies   Monet
couldn't do it better
at Giverny

                    at the Somme

light invades
turns one tree gold
a flash of azure
                    hapless prey
galahs garrulous
                    scream
concentric circles spread the surface
predators lurk deep
                    the Digger sinks
reflections

                    breathes

                    mud

Approach

I passed around him
gave him as wide a berth
as a dog come upon a seal

he was an omen, but
I couldn't quite catch
his drift, feared

passing on; saltwater
seeped from sand
about his feet

oozed between toes
that reminded me
of the crucifixion

even the light
played its part
startling white

foam circled my ankles
and I squinted into
the arse-end of day

asked him
where he was from
and when he said 'Here'

I didn't believe him

Unsaid

when I say *it feels like the afternoon*
and you say *that's because you got up early*
I hear censure in your voice
and all those unsaid things

and I don't, though I want to, say
it's not that – it's the light
and the distance between us widens,
the grey closes in …

Small Islands of Difference

night has stolen the day

slipped luminous
mother-of-pearl in its pocket

the tide sucks slap on the breakwater
strangers black against black

white last light from a line of
foam gleams on

the white of eye, the lift of brow
a greeting

turtles that pass
in the evening

a guitar, a bare bulb
harmony, small islands

of light. we live
in the shadows

understanding is
all, encompasses

all you could name:
charts, journals, the sextant

to navigate difference
let us sit side by side

here
on fine pandana matting

This Is How It Feels …

It is a freight train racing towards a washed-out bridge
a nor'west gale battering the weeping elm.

It is an astronaut in an anti-gravity chamber
a kick a punch from young thugs, after your wallet is stolen.

It is a child waking to find the nightmare real.
It is a father not knowing what to say,

the tremble of a dog waiting for a stick,
discovering your parents are getting a divorce.

It is being accosted by the school bully.
It is finding your daughter is on the streets.

It is the sound of people singing in a shelter
the knock of a woman taking food to the old man down the block.

It is the tumble of used bricks for a patio
the crumble of yet another investment bank.

It is ancient sand erupting in the streets of suburbia.
It is the baby who won't wait to be born.

In July I Think of Him

your birthday

you, who thought you knew
me better than myself
know me no longer

though I know you, still
round and round like this globe
of apple

red for love and green
for loving, slice by slice, a name
carved in singular fashion

I count the death of years
in decades, in the heart of winter
the vacant place in mine

remains; your firstborn
older now than you
still I'm your daughter

same hair, fine and disobedient
the nails, the crooked middle finger
words punning to cliché

sun-glance on water: *shine on
harvest moon, January, February, June*

now July

In the bedroom, shadows scud ...

Congress

You swept me off my feet,
while men in summer suits parted
like a wave of Aegean blue,
their eyes locked upon us. And
the girl in me
wished I could pretend
you were my lover, bronzed and strong
and half my age, wild hair tied at the nape,
wide smile. Your hands

lifting me toward sun. I wanted them
to see that I was more
than pedantry, more
than awkward interjections. Perhaps
see them preen their greying heads,
tweak a silk cuff, posture

revise their view
of *that dreadful New Zealand*

woman

Convergence

My voice, his voice.
Finishing his sentences
like a long-time lover, languid,
anticipating the very breath, the essence,
among rumpled sheets – yellowed pages,
dermatome slices, tissue-thin. I decipher
random hieroglyphs, each depicting
his world view: mountains and passes,
in tense, in hue, naming …
                            Recall
that limitless Te Anau night:
black water,
magnesium-flare of celestial bodies
lying together
touching
            infinity

Loving You

the air folded back
giving passage to words
which struck
like the J Arthur Rank man

I cried in black and white
movies while you were gone –
la strada, wild strawberries

we pluck wild
raspberries now
at Skippers ghost town
a sweet-blooded reminder
that good things can last

more than a lifetime
the red juice stains our mouths
and our fingers

A Song Sung

The sweep of your spine is my undoing.

I trace its course through muscled banks,
lingering. Each thoracic hillock; inscribe its detail
on my tongue. The base a pool to quench,
first and last. Every element miraculous.

The entire curve a bow stroke,
a treble clef awash with quavers,
quivers, against which I meld,
melt, salt, spineless

Extraordinary Lightness

Matariki

yellow paring of moon
and Mars sharp

the predawn Stephens blue-black

nib-scratched holes of light
search out like pairing:

you a crescent stretched
more moon than Mars

my world the old moon
in your arms, I linger

birdsong
            stars extinguish

the slow creep of day

On Your Toes

Michaelangelo may have carved your toes from Carrara marble. Translucent. Fine-boned but flightless. Relics, rarely viewed in their naked state.

I see you as a boy, wriggling those toes in an X-ray machine inside the shoe shop. All dem bones dancing for you, like any trick-shop skeleton.

When first we met, your toes languished in *tan shoes*. I threatened to give you *pink shoe laces*, and watched while you blushed from head to neck.

You've always toed the line – never been a toe-rag – and when you're toey, you don't kick the cat, but, in your socks and sandals, keep a toehold on reality.

Perpetually cold, your toes sleep under my duvet, give a little nudge now and then, speak their own language. I'd have it no other way, and I tell you this.

Breakfast in Berlin

You offer me an orange on the cusp,
no longer taut and slick, nor zesty,
but crenated like an old man's skin;
around the calyx shrivelled brown,
that part that clung tenaciously
when young. You peel the fruit,
and tender half. I bite into pithy flesh,
and sweet juice flows,
wakes my taste buds.   Sweet, still
so sweet.

Love

Let me not on the marriage of old minds
cast aspersions. Love is not spent
when income shrinks; nor when bodies
twist and gnarl, all angled limbs and creaks;
nor when sleep at night eludes, yet makes
its presence felt by day. Love is in
the shouted word that falls upon deaf ears;
in the hand that rests upon my thigh;
in the gesture, in the gaze that lingers;
in the smile. It's in the waiting, while I
search for something safely placed
beyond recall. Love is two memories
making one; casting assertions.

I Too Have Loved

Can you see
the bones of it beneath the dour – the inner
skeleton light as a bird and as flighty?
Lighter now than ever. And flown.
Straight, pressing it was, threatening
to cut, pluck out his heart, devour

A kiss in the mist,
cold Dunedin night, discovering
warmth in unexpected
places. Invisible, we rose
above. Invented love
in our innocence. Ephemeral
as the butterfly beating wings
in my throat

while I remember
                    who I have been

… But you won't see the cellar deep
where I store my vintage
loves. Where I linger
when I'm lonely. Sure
to bolt the door against their leaving.

Notes

Many poems in this collection have been prompted by events in my life, real or imagined. But a number were initiated by reading the work of other poets and being inspired by the form or structure, a concept or idea, a memory stimulated, or the personal significance for me of a word or phrase.

Elizabeth Smither describes [p. 67 in *Words Chosen Carefully*, edited by Siobhan Harvey (Cape Catley Ltd, 2010)] her weekly poetry writing session 'with inspiring collections beside me ... I read and write until I have written five poems.' Workshops by Joanna Preston on "Reading for Writing" also encourage reading others' poetry as an aid to the creative process.

A few of my poems are deliberately close to the original, in conversation with it, as it were. I may have taken the point of view of a different character, or be responding to the central concept. Collections such as *Answering Back*, edited by Carol Ann Duffy (Picador, 2008), legitimise this type of dialogue. But most of my poems which have commenced in this manner have taken off along their own paths and are now so far from the stimulus as to be unrecognisable and not warrant acknowledgement – though I have done so here for interest's sake, so that the reader may seek out the source if so inclined.

Lemon Tree: After "Lemon Tree" by Landis Everson, from *The Best American Poetry* 2007 (Scribner Poetry, 2007).

Awakening: I wrote this poem after reading "As Close as it Gets" by Paul Henry, from *the slipped leash* (Seren, 2002).

Summer in Ossetia: Written in response to a Reuters photograph, published in *The Press*, from Tskhinvali, South Ossetia, after five days of fighting between Russia and Georgia.

Expiration: After Louise Oxley's "Voice Over", from *Best Australian Poetry* 2003 (University of Queensland Press, 2003).

Foundations: The Romans laid siege to Jews living on the mountain of Masada, in what is now Israel. After about one year, the Romans finally breached the fortress to find the 960 inhabitants, including women and children, had committed mass suicide.

Azimuth: On December 21, 2010, there was a total eclipse of the moon, the first at the summer solstice since 1638.

Leavening: After "Swineherd" by Eiléan Ní Chuilleanáin, from *The Second Voyage* (Gallery Press, 1986).

Re-vision: This poem is after Louise Glück's "Presque Isle", from *The Wild Iris* (the Ecco Press, 1992).

Giacometti's Fancy: Giacometti exhibition, Christchurch Art Gallery, 2007.

On Losing Her Way: Brian Turner's "Flutter" in *Just This* (Victoria University Press, 2009) moved me to write about my own contact with dementia.

Digging Deep: After Seamus Heaney's poem "Digging", from *Death of a Naturalist* (Faber & Faber, 1966).

Air Born: This poem recalls the death of a woman who slipped from the harness of a chute in a tandem jump on Coronet Peak some years ago. I wanted to give the woman voice. The parallels with David Beach's "Parachute", *Best New Zealand Poems* 2003 (Victoria University Press online), will be apparent.

Mrs Popper's Sunhat: After Michael Harlow's "The Tram Conductor's Blue Cap" in *The Tram Conductor's Blue Cap* (Auckland University Press, 2009).

After Shock: After "You: A Fragment" by Bill Manhire, *The Elaboration* (Square & Circle, 1972) and *Collected Poems* (Victoria University Press, 2001).

Moscow Underground: This poem is written after Carol Ann Duffy's "Rain", from *Rapture* (Picador, 2005). КРАСНОПРЕСНСКАЯ [Krasnopresnskaya] is the closest underground station to Chekhov's House Museum.

Wings: After "What Flight Meant" by Christopher Meredith, from *The Meaning of Flight* (Seren, 2005).

From the Dead: Interacting with the instillation, *Shaleket*, by Israeli artist Menasche Kadishman, in The Memory Void of the Jewish Museum, Berlin.

Odyssey: I wrote "Odyssey" after reading the prose poem "The Deer Trap" by John Montague, from *The Forward Book of Poetry* 2005 (Forward Ltd, 2005).

A Long Time Coming: This poem was written after reading "Talking Ghosts" by Paul Henry, from *slipped the leash* (Seren, 2002).

Eclipsed: French marshland is known as the 'marais'.

She-wolf: In conversation with "Sister" by Joanne Limburg (*Magma Poetry* 45, 2008).

The Best Money Could Buy: After "The Conway Stewart" by Seamus Heaney, from *Human Chain* (Faber & Faber, 2010).

Chekhov's Birthday: Written after reading Sarah Quigley's column in *The Press*, July 2 (my father's birthday), 2011, and having recently visited Chekhov's House Museum, in his 'tallboy' house on Sadovaya-Kudrinskaya Ulitsa, Moscow, where he lived with his mother and siblings for four to five years, practised medicine, wrote and met with his literary friends. Chekhov died aged forty-four years of tuberculosis.

Out of the Whiteness: After "The Wolf" by Brigit Pegeen Kelly, from *The Best American Poetry* 2005 (Scribner Poetry, 2005).

What Is Yet to Come:
i-iii   *The Heart of the Great Alone: Scott, Shackleton and Arctic Photography*, the Royal Collection 2010, Her Majesty Queen Elizabeth II, exhibition in the Robert McDougall Gallery, Christchurch, 2011.
i   Herbert Ponting, photographer on Scott's *Terra Nova* (1912-13), Ross Island, Antarctica – *The Freezing of the Sea*.
ii   Captain Oates of Scott's expedition walked out into the snow to his death (16 March 1912) – 'I am just going outside and may be some time.'
iii   Frank Hurley was the photographer aboard the *Endurance* on Shackleton's expedition (1915-16).
iv   104 relatives of those who died in the Mt Erebus disaster attended a ceremony at the koru memorial, in sight of the mountain, on 16 February, 2011.

Dawn Parade: Caranbirini Lagoon, Northern Territory, Australia, ANZAC Day, 2007.

The Weight of Calves: After "The Weight of Cows" by Mandy Coe, from *The Forward Book of Poetry* 2005 (Forward Ltd, 2005).

Approach: After "In My Country" by Jackie Kay, from *Other Lovers* (Bloodaxe, 1993). I have taken the point of view of the second character, a woman.

Small Islands of Difference: In Samoa, fine pandana mats are brought out for dignitaries and special visitors to sit upon.

This Is How It Feels … This poem was written following the Christchurch earthquake, September 4, 2010. It uses the style and the structure of "What It Feels Like" by Brendan Ryan, from *Best Australian Poetry* 2007 (University of Queensland Press, 2007).

In July I Think of Him: After Deborah Garrison's "She Thinks of Him on Her Birthday", from *A Working Girl Can't Win* (Modern Library, 2000).

Congress: After "New Made" by Sheenagh Pugh, in *Stonelight* (Seren, 1999).

Convergence: Gillian Clarke's poem "Translation", from *Poetry* 1900-2000: *One hundred poets from Wales* edited by Meic Stephens (Library of Wales, 2007). At the time, I was affected by having edited the memoir of Dr David Jennings (1899-1982), in many regards a pioneer medical practitioner and tramper in Otago/Southland, New Zealand. It was very easy to identify with him, being myself a doctor and someone in love with our southern scenery.

Love: After William Shakespeare's *"Sonnet 116"*.

Loving You: By 'the J Arthur Rank man', I refer to the man stripped to the waist who used to beat the enormous gong at the commencement of all J Arthur Rank Organisation movies. *La Strada* and *Wild Strawberries* are black-and-white movies directed by Ingmar Bergman.

A Song Sung: One of two poems written as love poems to little-praised portions of the anatomy, after reading "Your Feet/Love Poem" by Kate Middleton (no, not that one!) from *The Best Australian Poetry* 2004 (University of Queensland Press).

Extraordinary Lightness: Stephens was a brand of fountain pen ink; blue-black was the colour deemed most appropriate for use at school with dip pens, which had a tendency to scratch holes in paper in the hands of students learning 'joined-together writing'.

On Your Toes: The second of two poems written after reading "Your Feet/Love Poem" by Kate Middleton from *The Best Australian Poetry* 2004 (University of Queensland Press). "Pink Shoelaces" by Mark Grant, singer Dodie Stevens 1959 – refrain: *'He wears tan shoes with pink shoelaces...'* My poem also sets out to give meaning to clichés.

Breakfast in Berlin: The writing of this poem was inspired by reading Carol Ann Duffy's book, *Rapture* (Picador, 2005).

I Too Have Loved: After "Late Love" by Jackie Kay, from *Life Mask* (Bloodaxe, 2005). I have responded to the line: *'How dull the lot that are not in love.'*

Recent IP Poetry

Musefood, *Margaret Ruckert*
ISBN 9781921869969, AU$25

Flaubert's Drum, *Sugu Pillay*
ISBN 9781921869945, AU$25

Maisie and The Black Cat Band, *E A Gleeson*
ISBN 9781921869440, AU$25

Sound and Bundy, *Amelia Walker*
ISBN 9781921869365, AU$25

Letters to my Lover, *Heather Taylor Johnson*
ISBN 9781921869662, AU$25

Ultra Soundings, *Duncan Richardson*
ISBN 9781921869341, AU$25

Words Flower From One To Another, *Amelia Fielden and Saeko Ogi*
ISBN 9781921869587, AU$25

Water over Stone, *Laura Jan Shore*
ISBN 9781921869208, AU$25

Tongues of Ash, *Keith Westwater*
ISBN 9781921869266, AU$25

Men Briefly Explained, *Tim Jones*
ISBN 9781921869327, AU$25

For the latest from IP, please visit us online at
http://ipoz.biz/Store/Store.htm
*or contact us by **phone/fax** at 61 7 3324 9319 or 61 7 3395 0269*
or sales@ipoz.biz